TRANSPORTATION
THEN AND NOW

by Robin Nelson

first step nonfiction

Lerner Publications · Minneapolis

Transportation carries people from one place to another.

Transportation has changed over time.

Long ago, wagons moved
people across the country.

Now, trucks move people
and things from city to city.

Long ago, **streetcars** took people through the city.

Now, **subways** take people
under the city.

Long ago, ships took people
to find new lands.

Now, bigger ships carry
people to places they know.

Long ago, trains moved
along the tracks.

Now, trains race even faster across the land.

Long ago, the first car
was built.

Now, cars come in many colors and sizes.

Long ago, airplanes began
to fly in the sky.

Now, airplanes fly very high and far.

Long ago, people only
dreamed of **outer space**.

Now, **spaceships** take
us there.

Transportation Timeline

1804
The first steam engine on rails is used.

1786
The steamboat is invented.

1832
The first streetcar in Harlem, New York, was pulled by horses.

1903
The Wright Brothers take their first flight in an airplane.

1908
The Ford Model T automobile is introduced.

1904
New York City's subway opens.

1841
Families begin to travel west in covered wagons on the Oregon Trail.

1873
Cable streetcars first run in San Francisco, California.

1869
The first coast-to-coast railroad is completed.

1981
The first space shuttle is sent into space.

1936
The first Volkswagen Beetle is developed.

1969
People land on the Moon in a spacecraft.

Transportation Facts

 The Wright Brothers' first flight covered a distance less than the length of a space shuttle.

 The first boats were made out of hollowed-out tree trunks.

 The first steam engines were fueled by burning coal or wood.

 The price of the first Ford Model T in 1908 was $850. In 1925 the Model T cost less than $300.

The fastest train in the world is in Japan. It can go 186 miles per hour.

 The United States has sent people to the Moon six different times.

 The Concorde is the fastest passenger jet. It can fly 1,350 miles per hour.

Glossary

 outer space – everywhere outside our world. The stars are in space.

 spaceship – a machine that can travel in space

 streetcars – vehicles that run on rails and carry people on city streets

 subways – trains that travel through tunnels underground

 transportation – things that take people from one place to another

Index

Villa Duchesne/Oak Hill - Library

200023590

The photographs in this book are reproduced through the courtesy of: © Brown Brothers, front cover, p. 12 © Todd Strand/Independent Photo Service, pp. 2, 5, 13, 22 (bottom); © Bettmann/CORBIS, pp. 3, 8; © Denver Public Library, Western History Department, p. 4; © Nevada Historical Society, pp. 6, 22 (middle); © Robert B. Levine, pp. 7, 22 (second from bottom); © Carnival Cruise Lines, p. 9; © Southern Pacific Company, p. 10; © Photodisc, pp. 11, 17, 22 (second from top); © North Carolina Department of Commerce, p. 14; United Airlines, p. 15; © H. Armstrong Roberts/CORBIS, pp. 16, 22 (top).

Lerner Publications Company
A division of Lerner Publishing Group, Inc.
241 First Avenue North
Minneapolis, MN 55401 USA

For reading levels and more information, look up this title at www.lernerbooks.com.

Library of Congress Cataloging-in-Publication Data

Nelson, Robin, 1971–
    Transportation then and now / by Robin Nelson.
        p.   cm. — (First step nonfiction)
    Summary: Presents a brief look at how transportation has changed over the years.
    Includes index.
    ISBN-13: 978-0-8225-4636-8 (lib. bdg. : alk. paper)
    ISBN-10: 0-8225-4636-1 (lib. bdg. : alk. paper)
    1. Transportation—United States—History—Juvenile literature. [1. Transportation—History.] I. Title. II. Series.
HE203 .N39 2003
388'.0973—dc21   2002010678

Manufactured in the United States of America
16-46907-4654-11/20/2018